The
MENTAL HEALTH
TOOLBOX

PRACTICAL STRATEGIES FOR A BALANCED LIFE

R. Packer

2024

I. Introduction

In an era where mental health concerns are becoming more common and recognized, the need for effective management tools and approaches has never been greater. "The Mental Health Toolbox" is intended as a complete handbook to provide individuals with practical solutions for navigating the complexities of mental health difficulties. This book aims to empower readers by presenting them with a variety of tools and practices that may be used in everyday life to promote improved mental health.

Purpose of these Tools

"The Mental Health Toolbox" attempts to simplify mental health management by providing easily accessible and actionable tools that anyone may use. The primary goal is to offer readers with a toolkit that will help them cope with stress, manage emotions, and build resilience. By providing these tools, the book aims to promote proactive mental health practices and remove the stigma associated with getting help.

Mental health spans a wide range of ailments and challenges, from minor stress and worry to more serious disorders such as depression and PTSD. This book recognizes this variability and provides tools that address a variety of needs and conditions. Whether someone wants to manage modest stressors or get help with more complicated mental health difficulties, "The Mental Health Toolbox" seeks to be an instructive and helpful resource.

Importance of Mental Health Management

Effective mental health care is critical to overall well-being and quality of life. Just as we prioritize physical health through exercise and nutrition, we must also take care of our mental health. Mental health affects many aspects of our lives, including our relationships, work performance, and ability to deal with obstacles.

Many people in today's fast-paced and frequently stressful world struggle with mental health issues such as anxiety, depression, burnout, or trauma. Without adequate management measures, these difficulties can worsen, causing major interruptions in everyday operations and long-term health repercussions. By supporting mental health management, this book hopes to inspire people to take an active role in their own well-being.

Furthermore, effective mental health treatment can improve resilience—the ability to recover from setbacks and overcome adversity. Building resilience is similar to growing a muscle; it requires consistent practice and the correct tools. "The Mental Health Toolbox" provides these resources, allowing readers to build the coping skills and emotional agility required to navigate life's inevitable ups and downs.

Summary of Tools and Techniques Covered

"The Mental Health Toolbox" includes a diverse set of evidence-based and practical tools and practices. These tools are organized into several major areas:

1. Cognitive Techniques: Include Cognitive Behavioral Therapy (CBT) exercises, thought diaries, and cognitive restructuring. These approaches assist individuals in identifying and challenging negative thought patterns, so encouraging more optimistic and realistic thinking.

2. Emotional Regulation Strategies: This includes mindfulness practices, deep breathing exercises, and progressive muscular relaxation. These approaches assist people efficiently manage and regulate their emotions, lowering stress and improving emotional well-being.

3. Stress Management Techniques: These include time management tactics, relaxation techniques, and stress-relieving hobbies. These tools enable people to identify stress causes and take proactive steps to minimize stress levels.

4. Social and Interpersonal Skills: This section covers assertiveness training, communication methods, and how to create and maintain supportive relationships. These abilities are essential for building a strong support network and handling social interactions efficiently.

5. Lifestyle Factors: Examples include the necessity of sleep hygiene, nutrition for mental health, and the advantages of regular physical activity. These characteristics have a substantial impact on general mental health and are necessary components of a comprehensive approach to well-being.

6. <u>Professional Support and Resources</u>:
Advice on when and how to seek
professional help, information on various
types of mental health specialists, and how
to choose the correct therapist or
counselor.

7. <u>Building Resilience</u>: Strategies for
establishing a resilient attitude, learning
from setbacks, and fostering positivity and
thankfulness.

8. <u>Special Considerations</u>: Strategies for
managing unique mental health disorders,
dealing with trauma or bereavement, and
providing support to caregivers and loved
ones.

Each tool and method is supported by
useful recommendations, real-life
examples, and exercises that readers can
use in their own lives. The goal is to enable
people to take active roles in their mental
health journeys by providing them with the
knowledge and skills they need to thrive.

In conclusion, "The Mental Health Toolbox"
is more than simply a book; it is a
comprehensive resource that empowers
people to take control of their mental
health. The book's goal is to create a
proactive

approach to mental health management by providing practical tools and practices that increase resilience, improve emotional control. It emphasizes the significance of addressing mental health issues early on and provides readers with a road map for efficiently developing and maintaining their mental health toolkit.

II. Understanding Mental Health

Mental Health: Definition

A basic component of general well-being, mental health affects psychological, social, and emotional spheres of a person's existence. It is not just the absence of mental disease but also a condition of well-being in which people may achieve their own potential, manage the ordinary demands of life, work productively, and benefit their community.

The World Health Organization (WHO) defines mental health as "a state of well-being in which an individual realizes his or her own abilities, can cope with the normal stresses of life, can work productively and is able to make a contribution to his or her community".

This definition underlines several important elements:

Mental health is about feeling good and performing effectively in daily life. Realizing one's potential entails honing one's skills to their best degree.

Effective Coping entails appropriate management of stress and obstacles. Mental wellness helps people to be productive workers who significantly benefit society.

Understanding mental health means that it exists on a spectrum. At one extreme are ideal mental health and well-being marked by good emotions, resiliency, and good coping mechanisms. On the other side are mental health problems and diseases, which can affect a person's thoughts, feelings, and actions greatly and span minor to severe levels.

Typical Psychological Problems

Different and affecting people of various ages, ethnicities, and situations are mental health issues. Among the most often occurring mental disorders are:

1. Anxiety disorders are those in which too great worry, fear, or anxiety can impede daily life. Among the examples are specific phobias, social anxiety, panic disorder, and generalized anxiety disorder.

2. Depression is typified by constant melancholy, a loss of interest or pleasure in activities, and changes in sleep, food, or energy level. Among depressed disorders

are major ones like seasonal affective disorder, dysthymia (chronic depressed disorder), and major depression.

3. Extreme mood fluctuations spanning emotional highs (mania or hypomania) and lows (depression) characterize bipolar disorders. Under this group include cyclothymic disorder, bipolar I disorder, and bipolar II disorder.

4. Following a stressful incident like combat, natural disaster, or personal violence, Post-stressful Stress Disorder (PTSD) can strike. Among the symptoms could be nightmares, flashbacks, extreme anxiety, and obsessive thinking about the event.

5. The hallmark of Obsessive-Compulsive Disorder (OCD) is repeated, unwelcome thoughts (obsessions) and/or compulsive activities. Many times, these actions are taken to reduce tension or stop a supposed disaster.

6. The chronic mental illness known as Schizophrenia Spectrum Disorders is distinguished by hallucinations, delusions, disorganized thinking, and poor social functioning. Schizoaffective disease and

delusional disorder are two other illnesses falling under this range.

7. Eating disorders like anorexia nervosa, bulimia nervosa, and binge-eating disorder disrupt eating behaviors, body image, and emotions connected to food and weight.

8. Personality disorders comprise persistent patterns of behavior, cognition, and inner experience that differ greatly from the expectations of the individual's culture. Among these are antisocial personality disorder, narcissistic personality disorder, and borderline personality disorder.

9. Substance Use Disorders are those in which a person uses drugs or alcohol excessively, so seriously compromising everyday life, relationships, and general well-being.

These disorders range in degree and can be caused by environmental stresses, biological elements, hereditary inclination, and life events among other things. Crucially, many people have symptoms of more than one condition concurrently, which can confound diagnosis and therapy.

Stigma Regarding Mental Health

Stigma continues to be a major obstacle to mental health treatment and assistance even with increasing knowledge and advocacy initiatives. Stigma is the negative attitudes, beliefs, and assumptions that cause discrimination or marginalization of people with mental health disorders. This stigma can be ubiquitous and affect many facets of a person's life, including access to healthcare, work possibilities, and relationships.

Types Of Stigma:

Social stigma results from people with mental health issues being targets of prejudice and discrimination directed by others. Social exclusion, bullying, or peer, coworker, or even family member avoidance can follow from this.

Self-stigma, then, is the inwardized negative ideas and emotions that people with mental health issues could acquire. Feelings of guilt, poor self-esteem, and unwillingness to tell people about their illness or seek treatment can follow from this.

Stigma Causes:

Lack of knowledge or exposure causes many people to have misunderstandings and fear concerning mental disease. Attitudes can be stigmatized in part by fear of the unknown.

Media sometimes sensationalizes or erroneously presents mental health issues, therefore feeding preconceptions and misunderstandings.

Attitudes and views in societies might be influenced by cultural or religious beliefs on mental health.

Stigma Consequences:

Stigma can deter people from seeking mental health care or support systems out of concern for judgment or prejudice.

Stigma can sour ties and cause social isolation or friend, family, or coworker rejection.

Stigma may cause someone to have less chances for housing, work, or educational background.

Confronting Stigma:

Reducing stigma calls both group activities at several levels and:

Encouragement of proper knowledge of mental health, dispelling of preconceptions, and raising awareness of the frequency and variety of mental health disorders constitute education and awareness.

Supporting laws and initiatives aiming at inclusiveness, anti-discrimination, and equitable access to mental health care.

Encouraging honest talks about mental health, sharing personal experiences, and creating supportive surroundings inside families, businesses, and communities will help both personally and community engagement.

To sum up, knowing mental health is realizing its complex character and includes well-being, resilience, and the management of mental health disorders. Promoting acceptance, access to treatment, and general well-being for people and communities equally depends on addressing the stigma attached with mental illness. We can build a society where mental health is given top priority by raising awareness, dispelling preconceptions, and supporting

surroundings that let everyone feel
appreciated and supported on their road
toward mental well-being.

III. Constructing a Foundation

Establishing a strong basis for mental health means including behaviors that advance wellness, resilience, and a balanced way of life. The principles of self-care, the value of routines and structure, and mindfulness and its advantages for developing mental and emotional wellness are discussed in this part.

Foundations of Self-Care

Especially in times of stress or difficulty, self-care is the intentional acts done to preserve or enhance one's health and well-being. With an eye toward restoring and recharging energy levels, it includes activities that foster the mind, body, and spirit. Though personal tastes and needs will affect them greatly, self-care activities usually consist in:

frequent exercise, good eating habits, enough sleep, and preventative healthcare —that is, frequent check-ups, vaccinations— are among the activities that help to promote physical health and vitality.

Emotional self-care emphasizes on cultivating good emotions, properly controlling stress, and developing resilience. This could be participating in joyful hobbies or activities, using relaxation techniques (such as deep breathing or progressive muscular relaxation), and using artistic or journaling to convey emotions.

Mental self-care is keeping cognitive health and clarity. To control racing ideas or anxiety, practice mindfulness and relaxation techniques; pursue lifelong learning or intellectual interests; and find mental stimulation from puzzles, reading, or interesting discussions.

Social self-care stresses on building a feeling of belonging and supporting relationships. Spending time with loved ones, getting in touch with friends or community organizations, and looking for social support under trying circumstances can all be part of this.

Spiritual self-care emphasizes on connecting with one's values and beliefs, discovering meaning and direction in life, and thereby fostering inner peace and harmony. Practices might be meditation, prayer, going to religious or spiritual events, or participating in outdoor activities meant to help one feel connected to something more than themselves.

Value of Structured Routines

Routines and structure give a sense of consistency and predictability—qualities absolutely vital for mental and emotional health. Establishing and preserving routines can help people control stress, boost output, and improve general quality of living. Important advantages of organization and consistency consist in:

Understanding what to expect and having a strategy in place helps one lower uncertainty and anxiety. Routines offer one control over their surroundings and situation.

Routines enable people to prioritize activities and allocate their time efficiently, therefore enhancing their productivity and goal accomplishment.

Frequent routines help to promote good behaviors like consistent sleep patterns, balanced meals, frequent exercise, and self-care practices.

Routines can support good behaviors and habits including mindfulness practice, consistent physical activity, and introspection by means of reinforcement.

Support for Mental Health organization offers a structure for daily tasks, therefore encouraging a feeling of fulfillment and success. Especially in trying circumstances, this can help to improve self-esteem and attitude.

Establishing sensible goals, determining priorities, and developing regular patterns of behavior help one to create successful routines. Maintaining general structure requires flexibility to also allow for unanticipated changes or challenges.

Overview of Mindfulness's Advantages

Mindfulness is a mental exercise anchored in the idea of accepting the current moment with acceptance and free from judgment. It is purposefully bringing awareness of ideas, emotions, physical sensations, or the surroundings. One can practice mindfulness techniques formally—that is, in meditation—or informally—that is, in conscious eating, conscious walking.

The Benefits Of Mindfulness

Mindfulness practice has been demonstrated to improve the body's response to stressors and lower physiological signs of stress like cortisol levels.

Mindfulness helps people respond more skillfully to difficult circumstances and properly control their emotions by raising awareness of them and responses.

Mindfulness practice helps one to maintain attention and concentrate on tasks, therefore enhancing their capacity for cognitive performance and output.

Mindfulness helps one to develop self-awareness by means of a deeper awareness of their ideas, emotions, and actions, so encouraging personal development.

Regular mindfulness practice helps to build resilience by encouraging adaptive coping mechanisms and thereby lowering rumination or negative self-talk.

By raising awareness of the mind-body link and hence supporting general well-being, mindfulness helps to promote a comprehensive approach to health.

Forms Of Mindfulness Techniques:

Sitting silently, mindful meditation focuses attention on the breath, body sensations, or a particular object free from judgment. As ideas come to me, practitioners softly note them and refocus on the selected anchor.

A body scan is a technique whereby tension or discomfort is released by methodically focusing on various body areas.

Participating in physical activities mindfully—that instance, yoga, tai chi, or walking meditation—where attention is on the movement, breath, and feelings in the body.

By paying attention to the present moment experience with curiosity and non-judging, informal mindfulness can be brought into daily tasks such eating, cleaning, or commuting.

Including mindfulness into daily life can be transforming and give basis for more self-awareness, resilience, and general mental health. Mindfulness practice develops not only a technique but also a way of life over time—a conscious approach to live that improves the quality of every moment and advances a balanced and satisfying life.

Conclusion

Resilience, well-being, and good stress management all depend on a basis for mental health built from self-care, routines, and mindfulness. Those who give self-care habits that support social, emotional, and physical health top priority top priority for building a strong basis for mental well-being Establishing routines and structure provide stability and encourages good habits supporting general health and productivity. Including mindfulness practice improves awareness, emotional control, and resilience; it provides useful tools for more easily and clearly negotiating the demands of life.

All things considered, making investments in these fundamental behaviors prepares one for a balanced and contented existence in which one may flourish spiritually, emotionally, and psychologically. Through including mindfulness, rituals, and self-care into daily living, people enable themselves to actively control their mental health and create a sustainable road toward total well-being.

IV. Tools for Daily Management

Daily management of mental health calls for a proactive strategy combining several tools and strategies meant to improve emotional resilience, cognitive flexibility, and stress management ability. Three main categories of tools for everyday management— cognitive approaches, emotional control strategies, and stress management techniques—are investigated in this part.

1. Mental Strategies

Within Cognitive Behavioral Therapy (CBT), a generally accepted and successful therapeutic method, cognitive processes are basic instruments. These approaches concentrate on spotting and changing bad thought patterns that support maladaptive behavior and emotional pain.

1.1 Cognitive Behavioral Therapy: Fundamentals

Cognitive Behavioral Therapy (CBT) is a goal-oriented, methodical psychotherapy emphasizing the interactions among ideas,

emotions, and behaviors. It seeks to spot
and alter ineffective thought patterns and
actions that support emotional problems.

<u>Important CBT Key Principles:</u>

CBT holds that our emotional reactions and
conduct are much influenced by our
thoughts, beliefs, and interpretations.
Cognitive restructuring is the process of
spotting and confronting cognitive
distortions—irrational or unhelpful ideas—
then substituting more reasonable, realistic
ideas.

Encouragement of good activities that
generate enjoyment or a sense of success
helps people to participate in which case
their motivation and mood will be raised.
Teaches particular coping skills, problem-
solving tactics, and relaxation techniques
to help control stress and improve general
well-being.

<u>Ingredients of CBT Sessions:</u>

Therapist and client jointly select
particular therapeutic goals and evaluate
present patterns of thinking, emotions, and
behavior.
Clients come to identify typical cognitive
distortions including black-and-- white

thinking, catastrophizing, and overgeneralizing.
Using evidence-based strategies, clients are helped to question and reframe negative ideas.
Through behavioral experiments or homework assignments meant to acquire data either supporting or contradicting their preconceptions, clients test the validity of their ideas and views.
Emphasizes the need of creating plans to keep improvement and stop relapse following therapy.

Uses of CBT:

Research on CBT has been voluminous and it has shown great success in treating several mental health disorders, including:

Depression helps people challenge negative ideas about the future, the world, and themselves as well as promote behavioral engagement to help to raise mood.
Teaches cognitive restructuring, progressive exposure to fearful events, and relaxation strategies to help with too great worry and anxiety.

Focusses on processing traumatic experiences, challenging negative ideas about safety and trust, and supporting

adaptive coping methods in Post-Traumatic Stress Disorder (PTSD.
While encouraging good coping mechanisms and relapse prevention techniques, Substance Use Disorder addresses triggers, cravings, and underlying beliefs driving drug use.

CBT's efficiency

Studies repeatedly show how well CBT lowers symptoms of several mental health conditions and increases general functioning. It is utilized either alone as a stand-in treatment or in concert with drugs or other therapeutic modalities.

1.2 Exercises for Cognitive Restructuring

A fundamental CBT strategy called "cognitive restructuring" is spotting and challenging negative thought patterns (cognitive distortions) and substituting more reasonable and realistic ideas.

Steps in Cognitive Restructuring:

1. Pay close attention to ideas that fuel emotions of melancholy, worry, rage, or other unpleasantness.

2. Review the data both supporting and refuting the negative thinking. Inquire of yourself things such, "What evidence do I have that supports this thought? What evidence do I have that contradicts it?"

3. Generating Alternative Thoughts: Create more realistic and balanced ideas considering several viewpoints or explanations. If the perspective is "I always mess things up," for instance, a more reasonable one could be "I have made mistakes in the past, but I have also succeeded and learned from my experiences."

4. Examining the Alternative Views: Think about your reaction upon adopting the alternative view. See any changes in your conduct or feelings?
In five, Acknowledgment and reinforcement of the favorable changes in thinking patterns and emotions brought about by cognitive restructuring is important.

Illustrations of Cognitive Distortions:

Viewing events in extreme terms—e.g., success or failure, perfect or worthless—is known as all-or-nothing thinking.
Making broad judgments based on few data —that is, "I failed this test, so I'm a failure in everything"—is known as overgeneralization.

Assuming you know what others are thinking without hard data, or "they think I'm incompetent," is mind reading. Expecting the worst-case situation to occur —that is, "if I fail this interview, my life will be ruined"—is catastrophizing. Personalizing events beyond of your control or blaming personal shortcomings (e.g., "It's my fault my friend is upset") for unfavorable results.

Advantages of Cognitive Restructuring

By altering the way people view and react to events, helps individuals manage strong emotions. Reducing cognitive biases and emphasizing reasonable answers helps to create more effective problem-solving skills. By challenging negative self-perceptions and promoting a more balanced and positive self-view, strengthens Self-Esteem.

1.3 Thought Notes and Applications

In CBT, thought records are instruments for tracking and evaluating ideas, feelings, and actions connected to particular events. They enable people to recognize their own habits of thinking and grow in more adaptable responses.

<u>Elements of a Thought Record:</u>

1. Explain the particular circumstance or incident that set off the emotional reaction.
2. Track the automatic ideas you had in reaction to the circumstances. Usually brief and instinctive, these ideas reveal underlying ideas or assumptions.

3. List and score the degree of the feelings (e.g., anxiety, sadness, rage) you went through under the circumstances.

4. List any cognitive distortions—that instance, black-and- white thinking, overgeneralizing—that might be present in the automatic ideas.

5. Alternative Views: Create more realistic and balanced substitutes for the first instinctful ideas.

6. Result: Consider how emotions and actions are affected when one replaces the automatic ideas with other ones. See any changes in your capacity to cope or sense of anxiety?

Example of a Thought Record:

Situation: Getting supervisor criticism on a performance assessment.

"I'm a failure. I'll never succeed in this job," automatic thought says.

Anxiety (8/10), then melancholy (5/10).

Cognitive distortions include overgeneralizing and all-or-nothing thinking.

Alternative Thought: "Receiving feedback is an opportunity for development. I have strengths and areas for improvement, and I can learn from this experience to enhance my performance."

Result: Lower anxiety (4/10), more drive to get helpful criticism and raise performance level.

<u>Advantages of Thought Records</u>

Helps people become more conscious of automatic ideas and their effects on emotions and actions.
Encouragement of cognitive flexibility helps one to grow in alternate viewpoints and more flexible approaches of thinking.
Through the challenge of cognitive distortions and development of alternative ideas, people can adjust their response to demanding circumstances.

2. Control Emotion

Emotional regulation is the capacity to control and react to feelings in a productive and healthy way. Good emotional control abilities help to build resilience, lower emotional stress, and improve general well-being.

2.1 Recognizing Feelings

Description: First identification and understanding of emotions is absolutely essential before one can properly control them. Complex psychological and physiological states, emotions include subjective sensations, physiological reactions, and behavioral responses.

Common Emotions:

Often in response to perceived threat, injustice, or frustration, **anger** is the feeling of annoyance or animosity.
Often in response to loss, disappointment, or disappointed expectations, **sadness** —that is, grief, unhappiness—is experienced.
Often in response to uncertainty, danger, or possible threat, **anxiety**—that is, a feeling of worry, fear, or apprehension—results.

Often in response to good experiences, successes, or relationships, **happiness** is a feeling of joy, contentment, or satisfaction.
Often in response to actual or imagined danger or threat, **Fear** causes anxiety or anguish.

Advantages of Recognizing Emotions

Identifying and categorizing emotions helps one become more self-aware of their own experiences and responses.
Better communication helps people to clearly express their wants and emotions to others, therefore promoting better relationships.
First step in learning to properly control and regulate emotions is awareness of them.

2.2 Techniques for Emotional Control

Strategies for emotional regulation are those tools and abilities people can employ to regulate their emotional reactions.

Effective Strategies Consist of:

1. Exercises for Breath

Deep breathing from the diaphragm helps the body to relax by means of slow, deep

breaths, therefore lowering physiological
arousal.
Several times, inhale for a count of four,
hold for four, exhale for four, and then hold
for four.
Focus on the sensation of breathing—
inhaling and exhaling—while releasing from
conflicting ideas.

2. Progressive Muscle Relaxation (PMR) :

Tensing and relaxing muscular groups
methodically across the body, PMR releases
physical tension and encourages
relaxation.
Start by tensing muscles tightly—that is,
fists, arms, shoulders—for a few seconds,
then release and observe the change in
feeling as muscles loosen.
Reduces muscle tension, decreases stress
hormones, and advances general relaxation
and well-being.

3. Mindfulness Meditation:

Mindfulness meditation is openly,
curiously, and with acceptance paying
attention to the present moment.
Improves awareness of ideas, feelings, and
physical sensations; helps one relax and
reduce tension; sharpens concentration
and attention.

4. Journaling and expressive writing:

Description: Writes about ideas, emotions, and events free from censoring or evaluation.
Benefits include a good release for emotions, encouragement of self-reflection and insight, and improvement of emotional processing and control.

5. Participating in creative outlets:

Art therapy is the creative expression and processing of emotions and ideas made possible by using art materials.
Using music to provoke and control emotions, therefore fostering relaxation and emotional well-being, is known as Music Therapy.

2.3 Expensive Journaling and Writing

Therapeutic approaches including writing about ideas, emotions, and experiences are expressive writing and journaling. These techniques help in emotional expression, introspection, and processing of emotions.

Expressive writing and journaling provide benefits:

Particularly strong or overpowering emotions, Emotional Release offers a safe

and healthy way for expressing and organizing sentiments.
Encouragement of self-discovery, a better awareness of personal events, and insight into ideas and actions helps one develop. Through externalizing and processing emotions through writing, stress reduces emotional arousal and physiological stress reactions.

Improved problem-solving enables cognitive processing of challenging circumstances, therefore guiding people toward perspective and adaptive coping mechanisms.

<u>Pointers for Good Journaling</u>:

Set aside specific time every day or week to journal, therefore forming a habit and obtaining long-term advantages.
Write candidly and honestly about ideas, feelings, and events free from censoring or self-judging.
Instead of emphasizing the result or perfection of writing, focus on process and pay attention to the way one expresses emotions.

Use specific questions or writing prompts to direct thought and investigation of many facets of feelings and events.

2.4 Combining Strategies of Emotional Regulation

Good emotional control is combining techniques catered to personal tastes and demands. Regular application of these approaches helps people improve emotional resilience, control stress, and foster a better quality of living.

Example Situation:

Situation: Anxiety and overwhelm before a job presentation.

Emotion: Anxiety (8/10).

Strategies for Emotional Regulation:

Slow, deep breaths help to relax the nervous system and lower physiological arousal.
Tense and relax muscle groups (e.g., shoulders, hands) to remove physical tension and encourage relaxation in Progressive Muscle Relaxation.
Practice attentive breathing to help you to ground yourself in the present and lower anxiety.
Journal about worry, worries over the presentation, and techniques to properly control stress while expressive writing.

The result is lower anxiety (4/10), more peace and preparedness to approach the presentation with more confidence.

3. Anxiety Control

In daily life, people naturally react to demands or problems by means of stress. Good stress management is the awareness of stressors, application of techniques to lower stress, and strengthening of resilience to face difficulty.

3.1 Stress Awareness and Triggers

Description: Stress awareness is the recognition of personal stresses, awareness of the indicators and symptoms of stress, and identification of the triggers causing stress reactions.

Common Stress Indices:

Physical complaints include headaches, muscular tension, tiredness, digestive issues.
Emotional: anxiety, impatience, mood swings, depression, feeling overburdened.
Cognitive: Problems focusing, racing ideas, memory loss.
Behavioral changes in hunger, disturbed sleep, social disengagement, more drug use —that is, alcohol and smoke.

<u>Spotting Personal Anxiety:</u>

Work-related: job expectations, deadlines, colleague conflicts.
Relationships: family strife, personal problems, caring obligations.
Financial: Debt, budgeting issues, trouble.
Medical issues, chronic illness, caring obligations define Health.
Moving, beginning a new job, significant life events (such as marriage or divorce) all fall under Life Transitions.

<u>Understanding Stress Triggers:</u>

Time constraints, crowded areas, noisy or chaotic surroundings.
Social conflicts with friends or relatives; social expectations; feeling evaluated or underlined.
Negative self-talk, perfectionism, unrealistically high standards are internal.

Physical: Bad sleep, insufficient food, little exercise.

3.2 Stress Reducing Strategies

Stress reduction strategies seek to balance both the psychological and physiological impacts of stress by encouraging relaxation and so relieving the tension.

<u>Effective Stress Reducing Strategies</u>
<u>Include:</u>

1. Mindfulness and Meditating:

Emphasizing present-moment awareness
free of judgment, mindfulness meditation
helps one relax and lowers stress.
Promote physical relaxation and stress
reduction by methodically scanning and
releasing tension from many areas of the
body in Body Scan Meditation.
Visualize peaceful pictures or scenarios to
induce relaxation and lower stress
responses in guided imagery.

2. Physical Action:

Engage in aerobic exercise including
swimming, jogging, or walking to release
endorphins, boost mood, and lower stress.
Combining physical postures, breathing
exercises, and meditation, yoga helps to
enhance flexibility, relaxation, and stress
release.

3. Techniques of Breathing:

Deep breathing from the diaphragm will
help the body to trigger its relaxation
reaction and lower stress.

Several times, inhale deeply for a count of four, hold for four, exhale for four, and hold for four.

4. PMR: Progressive Muscle Relaxation

To alleviate physical stress and encourage relaxation, methodically tense and relax muscle groups.
Benefits include lessening of stress hormones (such as cortisol), lessening of muscle tension, and general relaxation and well-being promoted.

5. Environment and Outdoor Pursuits:

Walking in a park, gardening, or just appreciating the natural surroundings will help you to connect with nature and lower stress and encourage relaxation.
Engage in outdoor pursuits as camping, riding, or hiking to revitalize emotionally and psychologically.

3.3 Techniques of Time Management

Good time management is task prioritization, activity organization, and productivity optimization that helps to lower stress and effectively reach goals.

Important Time Management Techniques Considered:

1. Eisenhower Matrix (quadrant approach) helps one to rank chores according to urgency and priority.

2. To direct attention and output, establish specific, measurable, achievable, relevant, and time-bound SMART goals.

3. To keep organization and output all around the day, set aside specific time blocks for chores, meetings, and breaks.

4. To combat procrastinating and keep momentum, divide chores into smaller, reasonable chunks and approach them methodically.

5. When suitable to maximize productivity and concentrate on high-priority projects, assign chores to others.

6. Preserve work-life balance and stop burnout, set limits on availability, personal time, and work hours.

7. Plan, calendar, task management app (e.g., Trello, Todoist), and time-tracking software tools help you to arrange chores and track advancement.

<u>Advantages of Good Time Management:</u>

Giving chores top priority and properly managing time helps to reduce overwhelm and stress related with deadlines and conflicting expectations.

By streamlining processes and concentrating on high-priority chores, improve productivity and goal accomplishment.

By juggling job obligations with personal and leisure interests, one enhances their work-life balance and general well-being and pleasure.

By establishing deadlines and benchmarks, one promotes responsibility and drive to finish projects effectively.

Including Stress Management Strategies

<u>An Example Scenario</u>

Situation: Feeling stressed physically (e.g., tension headaches, trouble focusing) and burdened with several deadlines at work.

<u>Techniques of Stress Management:</u>

To help you relax and concentrate, spend ten minutes in morning and before work mindfulness meditation.
During lunch break, go for a 20-minute stroll to help you relax, boost your mood, and increase general wellbeing.

Deep breathing techniques should be used all day to lower physiological arousal and control stress responses.

Using the Eisenhower Matrix, prioritize chores; set out particular time blocks for each; avoid multitasking to keep attention and output.

To relax, remove physical tension, and encourage peaceful sleep, practice PMR before bed.

Result
Reduced overload and physical signs of stress; improved focus and output; more general well-being and resilience.

Conclusion

To sum up, daily management of mental health depends on the instruments and approaches covered in this part: cognitive techniques, emotional control tactics, and stress management strategies. Those who regularly use these instruments and include them into daily activities can increase emotional resilience, cognitive flexibility, and stress management ability. These abilities not only enable people to more successfully negotiate obstacles and setbacks but also advance general well-being and quality of life. Using these skills to adopt a proactive attitude to mental health management creates a strong basis for continuous emotional wellness and personal development.

V. Social and Interpersonal Tools

Social connections and interpersonal relationships play a crucial role in mental health and well-being. This section explores various tools and strategies for building and maintaining healthy social connections, setting boundaries effectively, and developing assertiveness skills.

1. Building and Maintaining Social Connections

Social connections are fundamental to human happiness and psychological health. They provide emotional support, reduce feelings of loneliness and isolation, and contribute to a sense of belonging and purpose. Building and maintaining meaningful relationships require proactive effort and effective communication skills.

1.1 Importance of Social Connections

Definition: Social connections refer to the relationships and interactions individuals have with others, including friends, family, colleagues, and community members.

<u>Benefits of Social Connections:</u>

Emotional Support: Provides comfort, encouragement, and empathy during challenging times.

Reduced Stress and Anxiety: Promotes feelings of security, relaxation, and emotional well-being.

Improved Self-Esteem: Enhances feelings of self-worth and belonging through positive interactions and validation.

Enhanced Resilience: Strengthens coping mechanisms and adaptive responses to stress and adversity.

Sense of Purpose: Fosters a sense of belonging and connectedness to a larger community or social group.

1.2 Strategies for Building Social Connections

<u>Engaging in Social Activities:</u>

Joining Clubs or Groups: Participate in clubs, organizations, or interest groups aligned with personal hobbies or interests (e.g., book clubs, fitness classes).

Attending Social Events: Attend community events, workshops, or networking gatherings to meet new people and expand social circles.

1.2.1 Strengthening Existing Relationships:

Regular Communication: Stay in touch with friends and family through phone calls, video chats, or in-person meetings.

Quality Time: Schedule dedicated time for meaningful interactions and shared activities with loved ones.

1.2.2 Volunteering and Community Service:

Volunteer Opportunities: Engage in volunteer work or community service projects to connect with others who share similar values and goals.

1.2.3 Developing Social Skills:

Active Listening: Listen attentively to others, show empathy, and ask questions to demonstrate interest and understanding.

Effective Communication: Express thoughts, feelings, and needs clearly and respectfully; practice assertive communication (discussed further in section 3).

1.3 Nurturing Meaningful Connections

1.3.1 Authenticity and Vulnerability:

Being Genuine: Be yourself and show authenticity in interactions; share thoughts, feelings, and experiences honestly.

Building Trust: Foster trust through consistency, reliability, and mutual respect in relationships.

1.3.2 Cultivating Empathy:

Understanding Others: Practice empathy by recognizing and validating others' emotions and perspectives.

1.3.3 Conflict Resolution:

Handling Disagreements: Approach conflicts constructively by listening actively, seeking compromise, and focusing on solutions rather than blame.

1.4 Benefits of Meaningful Social Connections

1.4.1 Psychological Well-Being:

Reduced Loneliness: Alleviates feelings of isolation and loneliness, promoting emotional well-being and satisfaction.

Increased Happiness: Enhances mood and overall life satisfaction through positive social interactions and support.

1.4.2 Physical Health:

Stress Reduction: Lowers stress hormones (e.g., cortisol) and promotes relaxation, contributing to better physical health.

Immune Function: Boosts immune system function and resilience against illnesses and infections.

1.4.3 Longevity:

Studies show that individuals with strong social connections tend to live longer and healthier lives compared to those who are socially isolated.

2. Setting Boundaries

Setting boundaries is essential for maintaining healthy relationships, managing stress, and preserving personal well-being. Boundaries define acceptable limits in interactions with others, clarify expectations, and protect individual needs and preferences.

2.1 Understanding Boundaries

Definition: Boundaries are guidelines, rules, or limits that individuals set to protect their physical, emotional, and psychological well-being in relationships.

Types of Boundaries:

-Physical Boundaries: Personal space, touch preferences, and physical interactions with others.

Emotional Boundaries: Limitations on sharing personal feelings, vulnerabilities, and emotional responses with others.

Time Boundaries: Prioritizing personal time, commitments, and responsibilities to avoid overextending oneself.

Material Boundaries: Setting limits on sharing resources, possessions, or finances with others.

2.2 Importance of Setting Boundaries

Benefits of Healthy Boundaries:

Self-Care: Promotes self-respect and self-care by prioritizing personal needs, values, and well-being.

Respectful Relationships: Establishes mutual respect, trust, and understanding in interpersonal interactions.

Conflict Resolution: Facilitates conflict resolution and reduces misunderstandings or disagreements in relationships.

Reduced Stress: Minimizes stress from overcommitment, emotional strain, or unhealthy relationship dynamics.

2.3 Strategies for Setting Boundaries

2.3.1 Self-Awareness and Reflection:

Identify Personal Needs: Reflect on personal values, preferences, and limits to determine necessary boundaries.

Recognize Warning Signs: Pay attention to feelings of discomfort, resentment, or exhaustion as indicators of boundary violations.

2.3.2 Clear Communication:

Direct and Assertive Communication: Clearly articulate boundaries using "I" statements to express personal limits, expectations, and consequences.

Consistency: Maintain consistency in enforcing boundaries to establish clear expectations and promote respect.

2.3.3 Respect Others' Boundaries:

Mutual Understanding: Acknowledge and respect others' boundaries by listening actively and adjusting behavior accordingly.

Negotiation and Compromise: Collaborate on finding common ground and mutually acceptable solutions in relationships.

2.4 Overcoming Challenges in Boundary Setting

2.4.1 Guilt and Fear of Rejection:

Self-Validation: Validate personal needs and rights to establish boundaries that prioritize well-being.

Assertiveness Skills: Develop assertiveness skills to communicate boundaries confidently and respectfully.

2.4.2 Boundaries in Different Relationships:

Family Relationships: Navigate familial dynamics by setting boundaries around personal space, responsibilities, and communication.

Professional Boundaries: Establish boundaries in the workplace to maintain professionalism, manage workloads, and protect personal time.

2.5 Boundaries and Self-Care

2.5.1 Self-Care Practices:

Prioritize Needs: Make self-care a priority by setting boundaries around personal time, activities, and relationships.

Healthy Lifestyle: Maintain balance in physical, emotional, and social aspects of life to support overall well-being.

2.5.2 Reevaluating Boundaries:

Regularly reassess boundaries to accommodate changing needs, priorities, and relationship dynamics over time.

3. Assertiveness Training

Assertiveness is a communication skill that involves expressing thoughts, feelings, and needs confidently and respectfully while respecting the rights and boundaries of others. Assertiveness training empowers individuals to communicate effectively, advocate for themselves, and build healthier relationships.

3.1 Understanding Assertiveness

Definition: Assertiveness is the ability to communicate one's thoughts, feelings, and needs directly, honestly, and respectfully without violating the rights of others.

Key Aspects of Assertiveness:

Direct Communication: Clearly and directly communicate thoughts, feelings, and expectations using "I" statements.

Respectful Behavior: Maintain respect for oneself and others by acknowledging differing perspectives and boundaries.

Conflict Resolution: Address conflicts or disagreements constructively while promoting understanding and collaboration.

3.2 Benefits of Assertiveness

Benefits in Personal and Professional Settings:

Enhanced Self-Esteem: Promotes self-confidence and self-respect by expressing needs and preferences assertively.

Improved Communication: Facilitates clear and effective communication, reducing misunderstandings and conflicts in relationships.

Boundary Setting: Supports boundary setting by advocating for personal limits and expectations in interpersonal interactions.

Career Advancement: Contributes to professional growth by asserting opinions, negotiating effectively, and advocating for career goals.

3.3 Developing Assertiveness Skills

3.3.1 Assertive Communication Techniques:

"I" Statements: Express thoughts, feelings, and needs using assertive language (e.g., "I feel...when...because...").

Active Listening: Listen attentively to others' perspectives, acknowledge their viewpoints, and respond thoughtfully.

3.3.2 Assertive Body Language:

Eye Contact: Maintain consistent eye contact to convey confidence and sincerity in communication.

Posture and Gestures: Use open and relaxed body language to appear approachable and engaged in conversations.

3.3.3 Assertive Responses to Different Situations:

Requests and Offers: Respond assertively to requests or offers by clearly stating preferences, limitations, or alternative solutions.

Criticism and Feedback: Receive and respond to criticism or feedback assertively by acknowledging perspectives and discussing constructive solutions.

3.4 Overcoming Barriers to Assertiveness

3.4.1 Fear of Conflict or Rejection:

Positive Self-Talk: Challenge negative beliefs or self-doubt by affirming personal rights and strengths.

Gradual Exposure: Practice assertiveness in low-risk situations to build confidence and skills gradually.

3.4.2 Assertiveness in Different Contexts:

Personal Relationships: Assert personal boundaries, express feelings, and negotiate compromises in relationships.

Professional Settings: Advocate for professional
goals, assert opinions in meetings, and negotiate effectively with colleagues or clients.

3.5 Assertiveness and Emotional Regulation**

3.5.1 Emotional Awareness: Recognize and manage emotions effectively to communicate assertively and maintain composure in challenging situations.

3.5.2 Stress Management: Use assertiveness skills to address stressors, set priorities, and maintain balance between work and personal life.

Conclusion

In conclusion, social and interpersonal tools—building and maintaining social connections, setting boundaries, and assertiveness training—are essential for fostering healthy relationships, promoting self-respect, and enhancing overall well-being. By developing these skills, individuals can navigate social interactions confidently, communicate effectively, and cultivate meaningful connections that contribute to emotional resilience and fulfillment.

Embracing assertiveness and boundary-setting empowers individuals to advocate for their needs, protect their well-being, and foster mutually respectful relationships in personal and professional contexts. Incorporating these tools into daily life supports ongoing growth, self-discovery, and positive interactions with others, ultimately contributing to a balanced and fulfilling lifestyle.

VI. Lifestyle Factors

Lifestyle factors have a substantial impact on mental health and well-being, affecting cognitive performance, emotional resilience, and general quality of life. This section looks at the role of sleep hygiene, nutrition, and physical activity in supporting mental health and improving psychological well-being.

1. The Importance of Sleep Hygiene

Sleep hygiene encompasses techniques and behaviors that support good sleep and appropriate sleep patterns. Adequate sleep is critical for cognitive performance, emotional stability, and physical well-being.

1.1 Factors Impacting Sleep Hygiene

1.1.1 Sleeping Environment:

Optimal Conditions: Create a sleep-friendly atmosphere by providing a comfortable mattress, maintaining an acceptable room temperature, and minimizing noise and light disruption.

Sleep routine: Maintain a consistent sleep routine by going to bed and waking up at the same time every day, including weekends.

1.1.2 Sleep Routines:

Wind-Down Routine: Create a peaceful bedtime routine (e.g., reading, having a warm bath) to alert the body that it is time to sleep.

Limited Stimulants: Avoid coffee, nicotine, and electronic gadgets close to bedtime because these can disrupt sleep quality.

1.1.3 Stress Management

Mindful Practices: Reduce tension and promote relaxation before bedtime by practicing mindfulness meditation or deep breathing exercises.

Journaled: To cleanse your mind and relieve sleep anxiety, write down any thoughts or concerns you have.

1.2 Effects of Sleep on Mental Health

1.2.1 Cognitive Function:

Memory and Learning: Improves memory consolidation and cognitive ability, including learning and problem-solving abilities.

Attention and Focus: Enhances concentration, attention span, and mental flexibility.

1.2.2 Emotional Regulation:

Mood Stability: Enhances emotional resilience and stability by controlling emotions and lowering vulnerability to mood fluctuations.

Stress Reduction: Improves stress management skills and decreases cortisol levels, mitigating the effects of stress on mental health.

1.2.3. Physical Health:

Immune Function: Enhances immune system function, decreasing susceptibility to infections and diseases.

Metabolic Health: Regulates appetite hormones (such as ghrelin and leptin), lowering cravings and encouraging healthy eating habits.

1.3 Strategies to Improve Sleep Hygiene

1.3.1 Setting Up a Bedtime Routine:

Consistent Schedule: Maintain a consistent sleep-wake cycle to regulate circadian rhythms and increase sleep quality.

Relaxation Techniques: Prior to going to bed, practice relaxation techniques including progressive muscle relaxation and guided visualization.

1.3.2 Establishing a Sleep-Conducive Environment:

Comfortable Bedding: Purchase a supportive mattress, pillows, and bedding to improve comfort and encourage peaceful sleep.

Limiting Stimuli: Reduce your exposure to devices and bright lights before bedtime to help melatonin generation and improve sleep onset.

1.3.3 Handling Stress and Anxiety:

Stress Reduction: To relax and prepare for sleep, try stress-relieving activities like yoga, meditation, or deep breathing techniques.

2. Nutrition's Effect on Mental Health

Nutrition has a significant impact on mental health, altering brain function, mood regulation, and overall psychological wellbeing. A well-balanced diet contains necessary nutrients that promote cognitive function and emotional stability.

2.1 Nutrients Required for Mental Health

2.1.1 Omega-3 Fatty Acids:

Sources: Found in fatty fish (such as salmon and mackerel), flaxseeds, chia seeds, and walnuts.

Benefits: Promotes brain health, improves neurotransmitter function, and lowers the inflammation associated with mood disorders.

2.1.2 B Vitamins:

Sources: Found in whole grains, leafy greens, dairy products, and lean meats.

Benefits: It is necessary for energy generation, neurotransmitter synthesis (e.g., serotonin, dopamine), and stress management.

2.1.3 Antioxidants :

Sources: It is found in fruits (such as berries and citrus fruits), vegetables (such as spinach and kale), and nuts (such as almonds and pecans).

Benefits: Prevents oxidative stress in brain cells, improves cognitive function, and enhances mood stability.

2.2 Effects of Diet on Mental Health

2.2.1: Mood Regulation

Serotonin Production: Promotes serotonin production, a neurotransmitter that controls mood, sleep, and hunger.

Stress Response: Modifies stress response pathways and increases resilience to psychological stressors.

2.2.2 Cognitive Function :

Memory and Learning: Enhances cognitive processes like memory retention, learning capacity, and information processing speed.

Focus and Concentration: Enhances attention span, concentration, and mental clarity.

2.2.3 Gut-Brain Axis:

Microbiome Health: Promotes gut microbiota diversity, which influences mood regulation and mental health.

Inflammation: Reduces systemic inflammation, which is linked to mood disorders and cognitive impairment.

2.3 Tips for Keeping a Healthy Diet

2.3.1: Balanced Meals

Foods that are nutrient dense: Include a variety of fruits, vegetables, whole grains, lean meats, and healthy fats in your daily diet.

Portion Control: Mindful eating and portion control can help you maintain a balanced calorie intake and improve metabolic health.

2.3.2 Hydration:

Water intake: Stay hydrated by drinking enough water throughout the day, as dehydration can impair cognitive performance and mood.

2.3.3 Meal Plan:

Preparation: Plan meals and snacks ahead of time to make healthier options more accessible and reduce dependency on processed foods.

<u>2.3.4 Mindful Eating</u> :

Awareness: Pay attention to hunger and fullness cues, savor flavors, and avoid distractions (such as screens) when eating.

3. Physical Exercise and its Benefits

Physical exercise is not only good for your body, but it also helps you feel better, regulate your mood, and improve your cognitive function. Regular exercise improves brain function, lowers stress, and raises general quality of life.

3.1 The Psychological Benefits of Exercise

<u>3.1. Mood Enhancement:</u>

Endorphin Release: Promotes the release of endorphins, which are neurotransmitters that increase sensations of happiness and well-being.

Stress Reduction: Lowers cortisol levels, which reduces physiological stress responses and promotes relaxation.

<u>3.1.2 Anxiety Control:</u>

Calming Effect: Reduces anxiety symptoms by inducing relaxation, diverting attention away from problems, and increasing emotional resilience.

3.1.3 Depression Treatment:

Neurotransmitter Regulation: Elevates levels of serotonin and dopamine, neurotransmitters involved in mood regulation and pleasure.

3.2 Cognitive Benefits of Exercise

3.2.1 Brain Health:

Improves cognitive function by increasing neuroplasticity, memory, and information processing speed.

3.2.2 Executive Functions: Enhances executive functions including decision-making, problem-solving, and cognitive flexibility.

3.3 Physical Health Advantages of Exercise

3.3.1 Cardiovascular Health :

Heart health: Improves cardiovascular fitness, lowers the risk of heart disease, and promotes circulation.

3.3.2 Metabolic Health :

Weight Management: Promotes weight reduction or maintenance by burning calories and raising metabolic rate.

Control Your Blood Sugar: Improves insulin sensitivity, lowering the risk of type 2 diabetes and metabolic syndrome.

3.4 Strategies for Implementing Physical Exercise

3.4.1 Categories of Exercise:

Aerobic Exercise: Exercises such as walking, jogging, cycling, or swimming can help increase cardiovascular fitness and endurance.

Strength Training: Incorporate resistance training exercises (e.g., weightlifting and bodyweight workouts) to increase muscle strength and metabolism.

3.4.2 Flexibility and Balance:

Stretching Exercises: Use stretching or yoga to increase flexibility, reduce muscle tension, and promote relaxation.

3.4.3 Interval Training:

High-Intensity Interval Training (HIIT): Alternate high-intensity exercise and recuperation periods to enhance cardiovascular benefits and calorie burn.

3.5: Exercise as a Lifestyle Choice

3.5.1 Consistency: Create a regular fitness regimen by scheduling sessions and creating attainable goals to maintain motivation and adherence.

3.5.2 Variation: To avoid boredom and target different muscle areas, mix up your routines by attempting new exercises or activities.

Conclusion

Finally, lifestyle factors such as sleep hygiene, nutrition, and physical activity have important roles in boosting mental health, improving cognitive performance, and supporting general well-being. Individuals who prioritize these areas of their lifestyle can enhance their mental and physical health, reduce stress, and increase resistance to life's obstacles.

Adopting appropriate sleep patterns, eating a well-balanced diet rich in necessary nutrients, and participating in regular physical activity all contribute to a comprehensive approach to mental health management. These lifestyle choices not only boost mood, cognitive performance, and emotional regulation, but they also promote a sense of empowerment and vigor in everyday life. Including these behaviors in a comprehensive self-care routine promotes long-term mental and physical heath, improves quality of life, and promotes sustained pleasure and contentment.

VII. Professional Support and Resources

Seeking professional help is an important step toward properly managing mental health difficulties. This section discusses when to seek professional help, the various types of mental health specialists available, and how to identify the correct therapist or counselor.

1. When to Get Professional Help

Recognizing when to seek professional help for mental health issues is critical for early intervention and effective treatment. While everyone suffers periodic stress or emotional challenges, certain indications and symptoms may suggest the need for professional help:

1.1: Persistent Symptoms:

Persistent melancholy or worry: Experiencing overwhelming feelings of melancholy, worry, or hopelessness that interfere with daily life.

Mood Swings: Sudden mood changes or severe emotional highs and lows that interfere with relationships or function.

Changes in Behavior: Observable changes in behavior, such as increased irritation, social disengagement, or difficulties concentrating.

1.2 Effects on Daily Functioning:

Impaired Functioning: Difficulty doing daily duties at work, school, or home due to emotional distress or mental health issues.

Relationship Difficulties: Stressed relationships with family, friends, or colleagues as a result of mood swings, impatience, or withdrawal.

1.3 Physical symptoms:

Unexplained Physical Symptoms: Physical symptoms (e.g., headaches, digestive disorders) that do not have a clear medical cause and may be related to stress or mental distress.

1.4 Substance Usage:

Increased Use of Substances: A greater reliance on alcohol, drugs, or other substances to cope with emotions or symptoms.

1.5 Traumatic Event:

Trauma: Experiencing a traumatic incident (e.g., loss of a loved one, physical or emotional abuse) that has a long-term impact on daily life and emotional health.

1.6 Suicidal Thoughts and Behaviors:

Suicidal Thoughts: Suicidal or self-harming thoughts, as well as participating in self-destructive acts that endanger one's life.

1.7 Lack of Improvement:

Lack of Improvement: Symptoms that continue despite attempts to manage them independently using self-help tactics or the support of friends and family.

2. Categories of Mental Health Professionals

Understanding the duties and qualifications of various mental health providers can help people make more educated decisions about obtaining professional treatment. A variety of experts specialize in treating mental health illnesses and improving emotional well-being:

2.1 Psychiatrist:

Role: Physicians who specialize in detecting and treating mental diseases.

Therapeutic Approaches: Prescribe drugs, conduct psychotherapy, and track therapeutic progress.

Conditions Treated: Manage serious mental diseases (e.g., schizophrenia, bipolar disorder) and other medication-related conditions.

2.2 Psychologist:

Role: Doctoral-level psychologists who assess and treat mental health issues.

Treatment Approaches: Offer psychotherapy (talk therapy), do psychological examinations, and specialize in certain treatment modalities (e.g., CBT, psychoanalysis).

2.3 Clinical Social Worker:

Role: Licensed professionals with master's degrees in social work (MSW) who offer counseling and support services.

Treatment Approaches: Provide psychotherapy, advocacy, and case management services, typically in clinical settings or community mental health agencies.

2.4 Licensed Professional Counselor (LPC):

Role: Counselors who have completed their master's degree in counseling psychology or a comparable discipline and are licensed to give therapy and support.

Treatment Approaches: Provide individual and group treatment, specialize in various modalities (such as CBT and mindfulness-based therapy), and address a wide spectrum of mental health difficulties.

2.5 Marital and Family Therapist (MFT):

Role: Focus on working with couples and families to resolve relationship issues and increase communication.

Treatment Approaches: Offer family therapy, couples counseling, and individual therapy to address relationship dynamics and mental health issues.

2.6 Psychiatric Nurse Practitioner (PMHNP):

Role: Advanced practice nurses who specialize in mental health treatment, including assessment, diagnosis, and medication management.

Treatment Approaches: Prescribe drugs, administer treatment, and work with other healthcare providers to coordinate holistic care.

<u>2.7 Counselor or Therapist Specialized in Specific Modalities:</u>

Specifications: Some therapists focus on certain methods or groups, such as trauma-informed therapy, LGBTQ+ affirming therapy, or child and adolescent counseling.

3. Choosing the Right Therapist or Counselor

Finding a therapist or counselor who understands your needs and preferences is critical to developing a good therapy relationship and attaining significant results. Consider the following tactics when looking for the perfect professional:

<u>3.1 Assessment of Personal Needs:</u>

Identify Goals: Clearly define your therapy goals, such as stress management, relationship improvement, or treating specific mental health issues.

Preferred method: Based on studies or previous experiences, decide on your preferred therapeutic method (e.g., cognitive-behavioral therapy, psychodynamic therapy).

3.2 Research and Referral:

On-line Resources: Use online directories (e.g., Psychology Today, GoodTherapy) to find therapists based on area, specialty, and insurance coverage.

Recommendations: Look for referrals from reputable healthcare practitioners, friends, or family members who have had excellent experiences with therapists.

3.3 Initial Consultation:

In-person or phone consultations: Schedule first sessions with possible therapists to learn about their approach, experience, and how they may help you reach your therapeutic goals.

Ask Questions: Find out about their therapeutic approach, treatment methods, experience with similar concerns, and fees or insurance coverage.

3.4 Considerations for Compatibility:

Personal Fit: Evaluate the therapist's communication style, demeanor, and capacity to foster a safe and supportive therapy environment.

Cultural competency: Evaluate a therapist's cultural competency and sensitivity to your history, values, and identity.

3.5 Insurance and Financial Issues:

Insurance Coverage: Confirm therapist involvement in your health insurance plan and understand any copayments, deductibles, or out-of-pocket expenses.

Affordability: Discuss prices, sliding scale alternatives, and any financial aid programs to ensure that therapy is affordable.

4. Evaluating Progress and Effectiveness.

Once therapy begins, keep track of your improvement and the effectiveness of the treatment. Effective therapy requires collaboration between you and your therapist, in which goals are created, progress is tracked, and adjustments are made as needed.

<u>4.1 Monitoring Emotional Wellbeing:</u>

Self-Reflection: Consider changes in mood, stress levels, and coping techniques in between treatment sessions.

Feedback: Tell your therapist what's going well and where changes are required.

<u>4.2 Goal Accomplished:</u>

Goal Setting: Work with your therapist to establish realistic and attainable therapy goals connected to mental health improvement.

Tracking Progress: Monitor your progress toward goals over time and recognize milestones or accomplishments along the way.

<u>4.3 Adjustments in Treatment:</u>

Open Communication: Continue to communicate with your therapist about any issues, obstacles, or changes in symptoms.

Therapeutic Alliance: Assess the therapeutic connection and whether your therapist makes you feel understood, supported, and valued.

5. More Resources and Support

In addition to treatment, think about using other mental health resources and support services to improve your well-being:

5.1 Support Groups:

Peer Support: Join support groups or peer-led organizations to foster a sense of connection and understanding among people facing similar issues.

5.2 Educational Resources:

Books and Workbooks: Look into self-help books, workbooks, or online resources that offer information and solutions for dealing with mental health issues on your own.

5.3 Crisis Support:

Hotlines and Helplines: Call crisis hotlines or helplines for quick assistance in times of emotional distress or crisis.

5.4 Community Resources:

Community Mental Health Centers: Seek out resources and programs provided by local community mental health centers or charitable groups.

Conclusion

Seeking professional help and utilizing mental health resources are important steps in managing mental health issues, improving emotional well-being, and increasing overall quality of life. Recognizing when to seek help, recognizing the roles of various mental health specialists, and actively participating in therapy all contribute to successful treatment outcomes and personal development.

Finding the proper therapist entails evaluating personal requirements, investigating possibilities, and developing a therapy relationship based on trust, communication, and mutual treatment goals.

Individuals who prioritize mental health care and seek appropriate support services can create resilience, successfully manage symptoms, and negotiate life's obstacles with greater confidence and well-being.

VIII. Building Resilience

Navigating life's obstacles, conquering hardship, and preserving mental health all depend on resilience—which is developed by To build emotional strength and resilience, this part looks at techniques to develop a resilient attitude, learn from mistakes, and practice thankfulness and optimism.

1. Cultivating a Resilient Mindset

Resilience is the ability to adjust favorably against stress, difficulty, or major life events. By means of deliberate activities and mental changes, one can acquire and enhance this ability:

1.1: Resilience:

Accept change and open yourself to adapt to fresh conditions or challenges.

Maintaining a good attitude, concentrate on chances for development and education in trying circumstances.

1.2 Techniques to Build Resilience

1.2.1 Self-awareness:

Acknowledge and grasp your feelings, ideas, and responses to stress or hardship.

List your own resilience-supporting personal strengths, values, and coping strategies.

1.2.2 Skills in Problem-Solving:

Develop your ability to solve problems so you may evaluate obstacles, create reasonable objectives, and apply plans to reach them.

To get over challenges, make use of resources, networks of support, and skill set.

1.2.3 Positive Self-Talk:

From an optimistic standpoint, work on a good inner dialogue and challenge limiting ideas or negative self-talk.

Setbacks should be seen as chances for education, personal improvement, and progress.

1.2.4 Flexibility and Adaptability

Accept change as inevitable aspect of life and modify plans or objectives in line with it.

Resilient behavior: Stay flexible under demanding or erratic circumstances and concentrate on answers instead of problems.

2. Learning from Mistakes

Although they are unavoidable aspects of life, setbacks and mistakes can also present excellent chances for development, education, and building of resilience:

2.1 Appreciating Failure as a Teaching Tool:

Change your perspective to one that sees possibilities for development and temporary setbacks as such.

Think back on obstacles to find lessons discovered, areas of strength used, and areas of personal development need.

2.2 Developing Solving Strategies:

Analyzing challenges: Objectively evaluate losses to identify areas for development, implications, and influencing elements.

Create plans to handle problems, lower risks, and apply workable answers using a Solution-oriented Approach.

2.3 Requesting Guidance and Support:

Lean on reliable friends, relatives, or mentors for support, guidance, and viewpoint.

See therapists, coaches, or mentors to create resilience-building methods and coping skills.

2.4 Dedication and Tenacity:

To recover from obstacles and keep on toward your objectives, develop tenacity, will, and resilience.

As necessary, goal reassessment, modify deadlines or goals while keeping attention on long-term goals and personal development.

3. Harping Positivity and Gratitude

Developing a good attitude and expressing thanks can help one become more resilient, have better emotional well-being, and develop their coping strategies against difficulties:

3.1 Advantages of Thanks:

Emotional Resilience: improves emotional resilience by turning the emphasis from problems to good features of life.

Encouragement of a feeling of gratitude and contentment helps to lower stress, anxiety, and depression.

3.2 Techniques for Fostering Appreciation:

3.2.1 Grateful Journaling:

Daily Work: Set aside time every day to list three things you appreciate and consider happy events or times of gratitude.

To increase the effect, pay close attention to specifics and emotions related with thanksgiving gestures.

3.2.2 Acts of Kindness:

Engage in actions of kindness or charity toward others to help to build empathy, connection, and gratitude.

Engage in community service events to help to improve the life of others.

3.2.3 Positive Affirmations:

Practice positive self-statements or affirmations to underline personal value, strengths, and successes.

Regular repetition of affirmations helps one to develop a strong attitude and boost self-confidence.

3.3 Encouraging a Good Attitude

To keep optimism and drive, especially in trying circumstances, pay attention to the favorable elements of events.

Resilient thinking is the challenge of negative ideas or self-limiting beliefs from realistic and hopeful angles.

3.4 Presence and Mindfulness:

Use mindfulness strategies (such as deep breathing or meditation) to keep grounded, lower tension, and improve awareness of thankfulness.

4. Combining Methods of Resilience-Building

Including resilience-building techniques into daily life helps to strengthen emotions, improve coping strategies, and support general well-being:

4.1 Daily Routines:

Create daily schedules include gratitude exercises, relaxation methods, and self-care activities etc.

Maintaining a balanced diet, consistent exercise program, and enough sleep will help you promote both physical and mental wellness.

4.2 Stress Management and Self-Care:

Stress Reduction: Add stress-reducing strategies (such as yoga or progressive muscular relaxation) to release tension and advance calm.

To foster self-esteem, resiliency, and emotional well-being, practice forgiveness and self-compassion.

4.3 Development and Lifelong Learning:

Seek lifetime learning opportunities, pastimes, or interests that improve resilience, creativity, and personal development.

Accept fresh difficulties or events as chances for education, development, and strengthening of resilience abilities.

Conclusion

Resilience is about developing an attitude of adaptability, learning from mistakes, and fostering in daily life thankfulness and optimism. Resilience abilities help people to properly negotiate difficulty, control stress, and preserve emotional well-being.

Accepting difficulties as chances for development, learning from mistakes, and cultivating thankfulness help to build psychological resilience and improve coping strategies. Including resilience-building techniques into regular activities helps one develop personally, increase mental toughness, and change their perspective of life. Resilience ultimately helps people to reach personal objectives, flourish in the face of difficulty, and lead a happy, strong life.

IX: Special Considerations

Understanding and managing specific diseases, living with trauma or sorrow, and supporting caregivers and loved ones are all parts of dealing with special issues in mental health. This section looks at effective techniques and tools for these distinct components of mental health care.

1. Managing Specific Mental Health Conditions

To effectively manage specific mental health diseases such as anxiety disorders, depression, and other psychiatric disorders, specialized approaches and extensive treatment programs are required.

1.1 Anxiety Disorders

Anxiety disorders include a wide spectrum of conditions marked by excessive concern, fear, and heightened arousal. Common kinds include generalized anxiety disorder (GAD), panic disorder, social anxiety disorder, and phobias.

1.1.1 Cognitive-Behavioral Therapy (CBT):

Cognitive Restructuring: Recognize and confront negative thought patterns that contribute to anxiety.

Exposure Therapy: is the gradual exposure to feared situations or stimuli in order to lessen anxiety responses and induce desensitization.

1.1.2 Medicine Management:

Antidepressants: SSRIs (Selective Serotonin Reuptake Inhibitors) and SNRIs (Serotonin-Norepinephrine Reuptake Inhibitors) are frequently used to treat anxiety symptoms.

Anxiolytics: Benzodiazepines can be used to treat severe anxiety symptoms temporarily, but long-term use is generally discouraged due to the risk of dependence.

1.1.3 Relaxation Methods:

Deep Breathing: Use diaphragmatic breathing to relax and lessen physiological symptoms of worry (e.g., fast heartbeat, shallow breathing).

Progressive Muscular Relaxation (PMR):

Alternately tighten and relax muscular groups to relieve stress and encourage relaxation.

1.1.4 Lifestyle Changes:

Stress Management: Practice stress-relieving activities like yoga, meditation, or mindfulness to improve coping mechanisms and lower anxiety levels.

Healthy Lifestyle: Eat a balanced diet, exercise regularly, and get enough sleep to promote your general well-being and mental health.

1.2 Depression:

Depression is a mental illness marked by persistent feelings of melancholy, lack of interest or pleasure in activities, and changes in sleep, food, or energy levels. Effective treatment usually includes a combination of therapy and medication:

1.2.1 Therapeutic Approaches:

Cognitive Behavioral Therapy (CBT): Target negative thought and behavioral patterns that contribute to depression symptoms.

Interpersonal Therapy (IPT): Improving interpersonal interactions and communication skills might help alleviate depression.

1.2.2 Antidepressant Treatment:

SSRIs: Selective Serotonin Reuptake Inhibitors boost serotonin levels in the brain, which improves mood and reduces depression symptoms.

SNRIs: Serotonin-Norepinephrine Reuptake Inhibitors boost serotonin and norepinephrine levels, alleviating depressive symptoms.

1.2.3 Supportive Interventions:

Support Groups: Join a peer support or therapy group to share your experiences, acquire insights, and be encouraged by others who are facing similar issues.

Self-Care Practices: To improve emotional well-being, incorporate self-care activities like relaxation techniques, hobbies, or mindfulness practices.

1.2.4 Lifestyle Changes:

Physical Activity: Get regular exercise to release endorphins, reduce stress, and boost your mood and energy levels.

Nutrition: Eat a well-balanced diet high in nutrients, omega-3 fatty acids, and antioxidants to promote brain health and mood regulation.

<u>1.3 Other Psychiatric Disorders:</u>

1.3.1: Bipolar Disorder: Manage and stabilize mood swings with mood stabilizers, antipsychotics, and psychotherapy (e.g., CBT, psycho-education).

1.3.2 Schizophrenia : Antipsychotic drugs, therapy, and support services customized to individual requirements can help treat psychotic symptoms (e.g., hallucinations, delusions).

2. Strategies for Dealing with Trauma or Grief

Experiencing trauma or bereavement can have a profound influence on one's mental health and wellbeing. Emotional processing and healing require effective coping techniques and support structures.

<u>2.1 Dealing with Trauma:</u>

Trauma-Informed Therapy: Try trauma-focused therapies like Eye Movement Desensitization and Reprocessing (EMDR) or Trauma-Focused Cognitive Behavioral Therapy (TF-CBT).

Grounding Techniques: Use grounding activities (such as mindfulness and sensory awareness) to stay present and handle uncomfortable emotions or flashbacks.

2.2 Grief Support:

Grief Counseling: Seek counseling or support groups to help you navigate the grieving process, express your emotions, and learn how to cope with loss.

Expressive Arts Therapy: Use creative outlets like painting, music, or writing to process grief, express emotions, and honor a loved one's memory.

2.3 Self-Care Practices:

Mindfulness and meditation: Practice mindfulness to improve self-awareness, reduce stress, and facilitate emotional healing.

Physical Activity: Try light exercise or outdoor activities to relieve stress, improve mood, and boost general well-being.

<u>2.4 Support Networks:</u>

Family and Friends: Turn to trusted loved ones for emotional support, companionship, and understanding during times of tragedy or sadness.

Peer Support Groups: Connect with people who have gone through similar losses or trauma to share your experiences, receive validation, and build a sense of belonging.

3. Help for Caregivers and Loved Ones

Caregivers play an important role in helping people with mental illnesses or trauma, providing necessary care, and facilitating recovery. It is critical to meet their specific demands and concerns.

<u>3.1 Caregivers' Stress and Burnout:</u>

Recognizing Signs: Look for symptoms of caregiver stress, such as weariness, impatience, and feelings of isolation or overload.

Self-Care Practices: Prioritize self-care activities such as relaxation techniques, hobbies, or respite care to avoid burnout and preserve overall wellness.

3.2 Education and Resources:

Info: Seek out information and resources on the specific mental health issue or trauma to better understand symptoms, treatment choices, and supportive tactics.

Support Networks: Join caregiver support groups or online forums to interact with others, discuss your experiences, and seek advice from peers or mental health specialists.

3.3 Communication and boundaries:

Open Communication: Communicate openly and honestly with the person getting care, sharing issues, treatment plans, and goals together.

Setting limits: Set clear limits to balance caregiving responsibilities with personal needs while ensuring physical and emotional well-being.

3.4 Professional Support:

Therapeutic Support: Seek therapy or counseling to help you process emotions, manage stress, and gain perspective on caregiving problems.

Respite Care: Arrange for respite care services so that caregivers can take breaks for rest, socialization, or personal pursuits.

4: Advocacy and Community Engagement

Advocacy and community participation are critical in raising awareness, eliminating stigma, and increasing access to mental health resources and support services:

4.1 Advocacy Initiatives:

Educational Campaigns: Encourage programs that educate the general public, healthcare practitioners, and policymakers about mental health challenges, treatment options, and available resources.

Policy Advocacy: Advocate for policies that improve mental health services, research funding, and access to care for individuals and families living with mental health conditions.

4.2 Community Support:

Local Resources: Look into neighborhood mental health clinics, nonprofit organizations, or faith-based groups that provide support groups, counseling services, or educational courses.

Volunteer Opportunities: Offer your time or skills to mental health organizations, advocacy groups, or crisis intervention programs to help individuals and families in need.

5: Personal Empowerment and Resilience Building

Empowering individuals and their support networks with knowledge, resources, and resilience-building tactics increases self-efficacy and improves overall well-being.

5.1 Education and Awareness:

Knowledge acquisition: Seek knowledge and resources on mental health disorders, coping skills, and

successful treatment options to help you make sound decisions.

5.2 Self Advocacy:

Voice Concerns: Communicate personal requirements, preferences, and treatment goals to healthcare practitioners, therapists, or support networks.

Assertiveness Abilities: Improve your assertiveness abilities to speak effectively, set limits, and negotiate healthcare or support systems.

5.3 Practices for Building Resilience

Positive Coping Strategies: Practice resilience-building activities such as mindfulness, gratitude, and self-care to improve emotional strength and adaptive coping methods.

Goal Setting: Set attainable goals for personal growth, recovery, or well-being, and celebrate accomplishments and progress along the way.

Conclusion

Special mental health considerations include treating unique diseases, dealing with trauma or bereavement, and assisting caregivers and loved ones. Tailored treatments for anxiety disorders, depression, and other psychiatric diseases that emphasize therapy, medication, and lifestyle changes are among the most effective strategies. Coping with trauma or bereavement entails using therapy approaches, self-care routines, and support networks to encourage healing and resilience.

To prevent burnout and sustain well-being, caregivers must be supported by addressing their educational, self-care, and community resource needs. Advocacy initiatives and community engagement are critical for raising awareness, eliminating stigma, and increasing access to mental health resources. We promote an awareness, support, and resilience culture in mental health treatment by empowering individuals and their support networks with knowledge, resilience-building methods, and compassionate support.